TRUMPET

101 HIT SONGS

T0087268

Available for
FLUTE, CLARINET, ALTO SAX, TENOR SAX, TRUMPET,
HORN, TROMBONE, VIOLIN, VIOLA, CELLO

ISBN 978-1-4950-7532-2

HAL•LEONARD®

7777 W. Bluemound Rd. P.O. Box 13819 Milwaukee, WI 53213

CONTENTS

ALL ABOUT THAT BASS

TRUMPET

Words and Music by KEVIN KADISH
and MEGHAN TRAINOR

AMAZED

TRUMPET

Words and Music by MARV GREEN,
CHRIS LINDSEY and AIMEE MAYO

Moderately slow

ALL OF ME

TRUMPET

Words and Music by JOHN STEPHENS
and TOBY GAD

1.
1st time D.C.
2nd Time Fine
2.
D.S. al Fine
(take 1st ending)

APOLOGIZE

TRUMPET

Words and Music by
RYAN TEDDER

BEAUTIFUL

TRUMPET

Words and Music by
LINDA PERRY

BAD DAY

TRUMPET

Words and Music by
DANIEL POWTER

D.S. al Coda
CODA

BAD ROMANCE

TRUMPET

Words and Music by STEFANI GERMANOTTA
and NADIR KHAYAT

BEAUTIFUL DAY

TRUMPET

Words by BONO
Music by U2

To Coda
1.
3
2.
D.S. al Coda
CODA

BEAUTIFUL IN MY EYES

TRUMPET

Words and Music by
JOSHUA KADISON

BECAUSE I LOVE YOU
(The Postman Song)

TRUMPET

Words and Music by
WARREN BROOKS

BELIEVE

TRUMPET

Words and Music by BRIAN HIGGINS,
STUART McLENNEN, PAUL BARRY,
STEPHEN TORCH, MATT GRAY
and TIM POWELL

BUTTERFLY KISSES

TRUMPET

Words and Music by BOB CARLISLE
and RANDY THOMAS

BRAVE

TRUMPET

Words and Music by SARA BAREILLES
and JACK ANTONOFF

To Coda
D.S. al Coda
CODA

BREAKAWAY

from THE PRINCESS DIARIES 2: ROYAL ENGAGEMENT

TRUMPET

Words and Music by BRIDGET BENENATE,
AVRIL LAVIGNE and MATTHEW GERRARD

Slowly, in 2

BREATHE

TRUMPET

Words and Music by HOLLY LAMAR
and STEPHANIE BENTLEY

Moderately fast

To Coda
1.
2.
D.S. al Coda
CODA
2

CALL ME MAYBE

TRUMPET

Words and Music by CARLY RAE JEPSEN,
JOSHUA RAMSAY and TAVISH CROWE

Moderately

To Coda
D.S. al Coda
(no repeat)
CODA

CANDLE IN THE WIND 1997

TRUMPET

Words and Music by ELTON JOHN
and BERNIE TAUPIN

CHANGE THE WORLD

featured on the Motion Picture Soundtrack PHENOMENON

TRUMPET

Words and Music by WAYNE KIRKPATRICK,
GORDON KENNEDY and TOMMY SIMS

Moderately

CHASING CARS

TRUMPET

Words and Music by GARY LIGHTBODY,
TOM SIMPSON, PAUL WILSON,
JONATHAN QUINN and NATHAN CONNOLLY

THE CLIMB

from HANNAH MONTANA: THE MOVIE

TRUMPET

Words and Music by JESSI ALEXANDER
and JON MABE

CLOCKS

TRUMPET

Words and Music by GUY BERRYMAN, JON BUCKLAND, WILL CHAMPION and CHRIS MARTIN

DON'T KNOW WHY

TRUMPET

Words and Music by
JESSE HARRIS

Moderately slow

COUNTDOWN

TRUMPET

Words and Music by BEYONCÉ KNOWLES,
CAINON LAMB, JULIE FROST, MICHAEL BIVINS,
ESTHER DEAN, TERIUS NASH, SHEA TAYLOR,
NATHAN MORRIS and WANYA MORRIS

2nd time, D.C. al Coda
CODA

CRUISE

TRUMPET

Words and Music by CHASE RICE,
TYLER HUBBARD, BRIAN KELLEY,
JOEY MOI and JESSE RICE

Moderately, in 2

To Coda
1.
2.
D.S. al Coda
CODA
3

CRYIN'

TRUMPET

Words and Music by STEVEN TYLER,
JOE PERRY and TAYLOR RHODES

Moderately slow, in 2

Fine
1.
2.
D.S. al Fine

DIE A HAPPY MAN

TRUMPET

Words and Music by THOMAS RHETT,
JOE SPARGUR and SEAN DOUGLAS

Moderately slow

1.
2.

DILEMMA

TRUMPET

Words and Music by CORNELL HAYNES,
ANTWON MAKER, KENNETH GAMBLE
and BUNNY SIGLER

Fine
2nd time, D.S. al Fine

DRIFT AWAY

TRUMPET

Words and Music by
MENTOR WILLIAMS

FIELDS OF GOLD

TRUMPET

Music and Lyrics by
STING

DROPS OF JUPITER
(Tell Me)

TRUMPET

Words and Music by PAT MONAHAN,
JAMES STAFFORD, ROBERT HOTCHKISS,
CHARLES COLIN and SCOTT UNDERWOOD

D.S. al Coda
CODA

FALLIN'

TRUMPET

Words and Music by
ALICIA KEYS

1., 2.
3.

FIREWORK

TRUMPET

Words and Music by KATY PERRY,
MIKKEL ERIKSEN, TOR ERIK HERMANSEN,
ESTHER DEAN and SANDY WILHELM

Moderately

To Coda
D.S. al Coda
CODA

FOOLISH GAMES

TRUMPET

Words and Music by
JEWEL KILCHER

3
3
3
3

FOREVER AND FOR ALWAYS

TRUMPET

Words and Music by SHANIA TWAIN
and R.J. LANGE

Moderately, in 2

1.
2.

FRIENDS IN LOW PLACES

TRUMPET

Words and Music by DeWAYNE BLACKWELL
and EARL BUD LEE

Moderately

FROM A DISTANCE

TRUMPET

Words and Music by
JULIE GOLD

GENIE IN A BOTTLE

TRUMPET

Words and Music by STEVE KIPNER, DAVID FRANK and PAMELA SHEYNE

Moderately

1.
3
2.
To Coda
2nd time, D.S. al Coda
(take 2nd ending)
CODA

GET LUCKY

TRUMPET

Words and Music by THOMAS BANGALTER,
GUY MANUEL HOMEM CHRISTO, NILE RODGERS
and PHARRELL WILLIAMS

HOW TO SAVE A LIFE

TRUMPET

Words and Music by JOSEPH KING
and ISAAC SLADE

Moderately fast

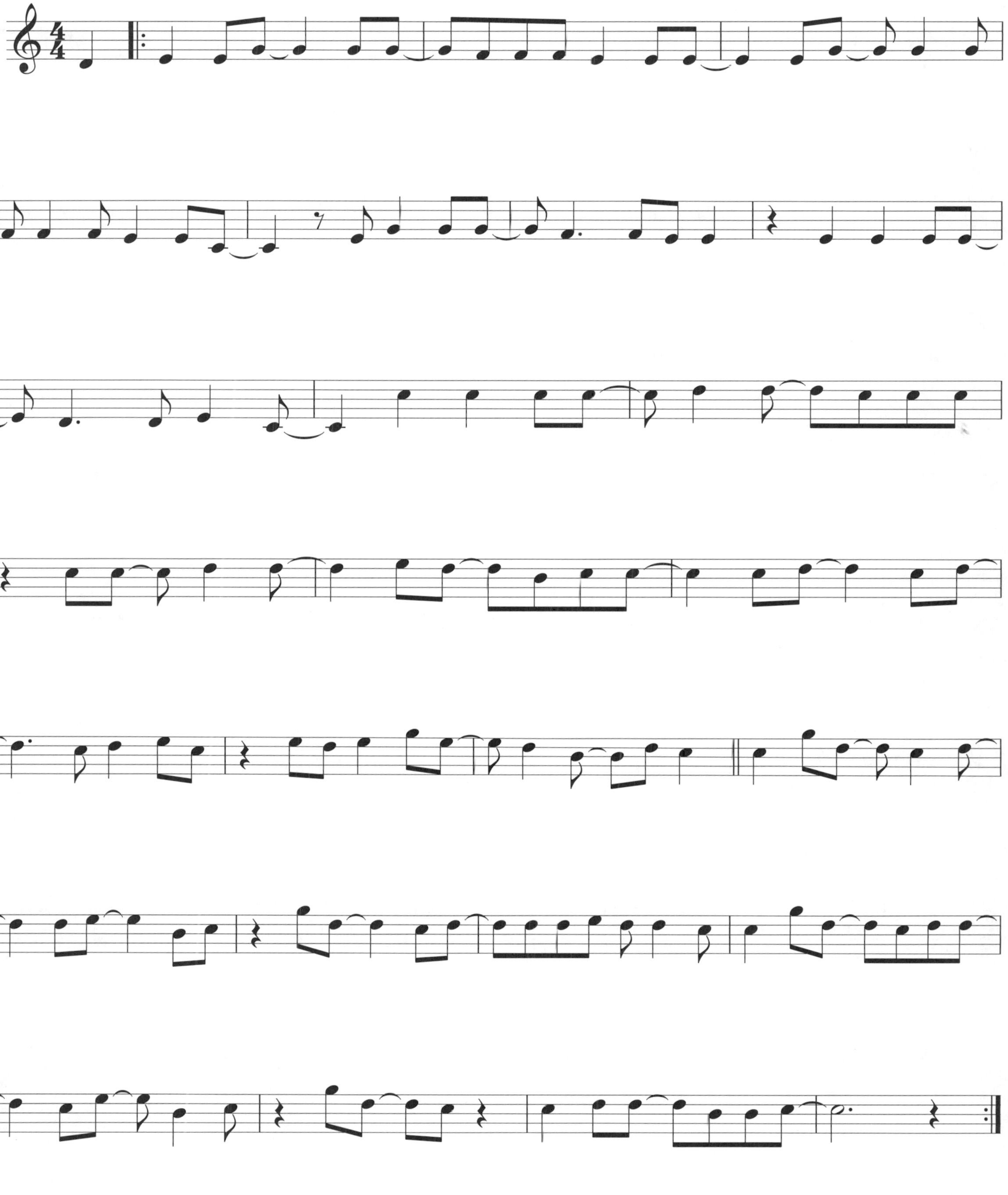

HELLO

TRUMPET

Words and Music by ADELE ADKINS
and GREG KURSTIN

Moderately slow

HERE AND NOW

TRUMPET

Words and Music by TERRY STEELE
and DAVID ELLIOT

To Coda
1.
2.
D.S. al Coda
CODA

HERO

TRUMPET

Words and Music by ENRIQUE IGLESIAS,
PAUL BARRY and MARK TAYLOR

Moderately slow

1.
2.
1., 2.
3.

HEY, SOUL SISTER

TRUMPET

Words and Music by PAT MONAHAN,
ESPEN LIND and AMUND BJORKLUND

To Coda
1.
2.
D.S. al Coda
CODA
1.
2.

HO HEY

TRUMPET

Words and Music by JEREMY FRAITES
and WESLEY SCHULTZ

Moderately slow, in 2

1.
Fine
2.
D.S. al Fine
(take 1st ending)

HOLD ON, WE'RE GOING HOME

TRUMPET

Words and Music by AUBREY GRAHAM,
PAUL JEFFERIES, NOAH SHEBIB,
JORDAN ULLMAN and MAJID AL-MASKATI

Moderately

1.
Fine
2.
1.
2.
D.S. al Fine
(take 1st ending)

HOME

TRUMPET

Words and Music by GREG HOLDEN
and DREW PEARSON

Moderately, in 2

THE HOUSE THAT BUILT ME

TRUMPET

Words and Music by TOM DOUGLAS
and ALLEN SHAMBLIN

Fine
D.S. al Fine

HOW AM I SUPPOSED TO LIVE WITHOUT YOU

TRUMPET

Words and Music by MICHAEL BOLTON
and DOUG JAMES

1.
2.

I FINALLY FOUND SOMEONE

from THE MIRROR HAS TWO FACES

TRUMPET

Words and Music by BARBRA STREISAND, MARVIN HAMLISCH, R.J. LANGE and BRYAN ADAMS

Moderately slow

Fine
D.S. al Fine

I GOTTA FEELING

TRUMPET

Words and Music by WILL ADAMS,
ALLAN PINEDA, JAIME GOMEZ, STACY FERGUSON,
DAVID GUETTA and FREDERIC RIESTERER

Moderately fast

1.
2.
To Coda
D.S. al Coda
(take repeat)
CODA

I KISSED A GIRL

TRUMPET

Words and Music by KATY PERRY,
CATHY DENNIS, MAX MARTIN
and LUKASZ GOTTWALD

Moderately

1.
Fine
2.
D.S. al Fine
(take 1st ending)

I SWEAR

TRUMPET

Words and Music by FRANK MYERS
and GARY BAKER

Moderately

I WILL REMEMBER YOU

Theme from THE BROTHERS McMULLEN

TRUMPET

Words and Music by SARAH McLACHLAN,
SEAMUS EGAN and DAVE MERENDA

Moderately slow

JAR OF HEARTS

TRUMPET

Words and Music by BARRETT YERETSIAN,
CHRISTINA PERRI and DREW LAWRENCE

Moderately slow

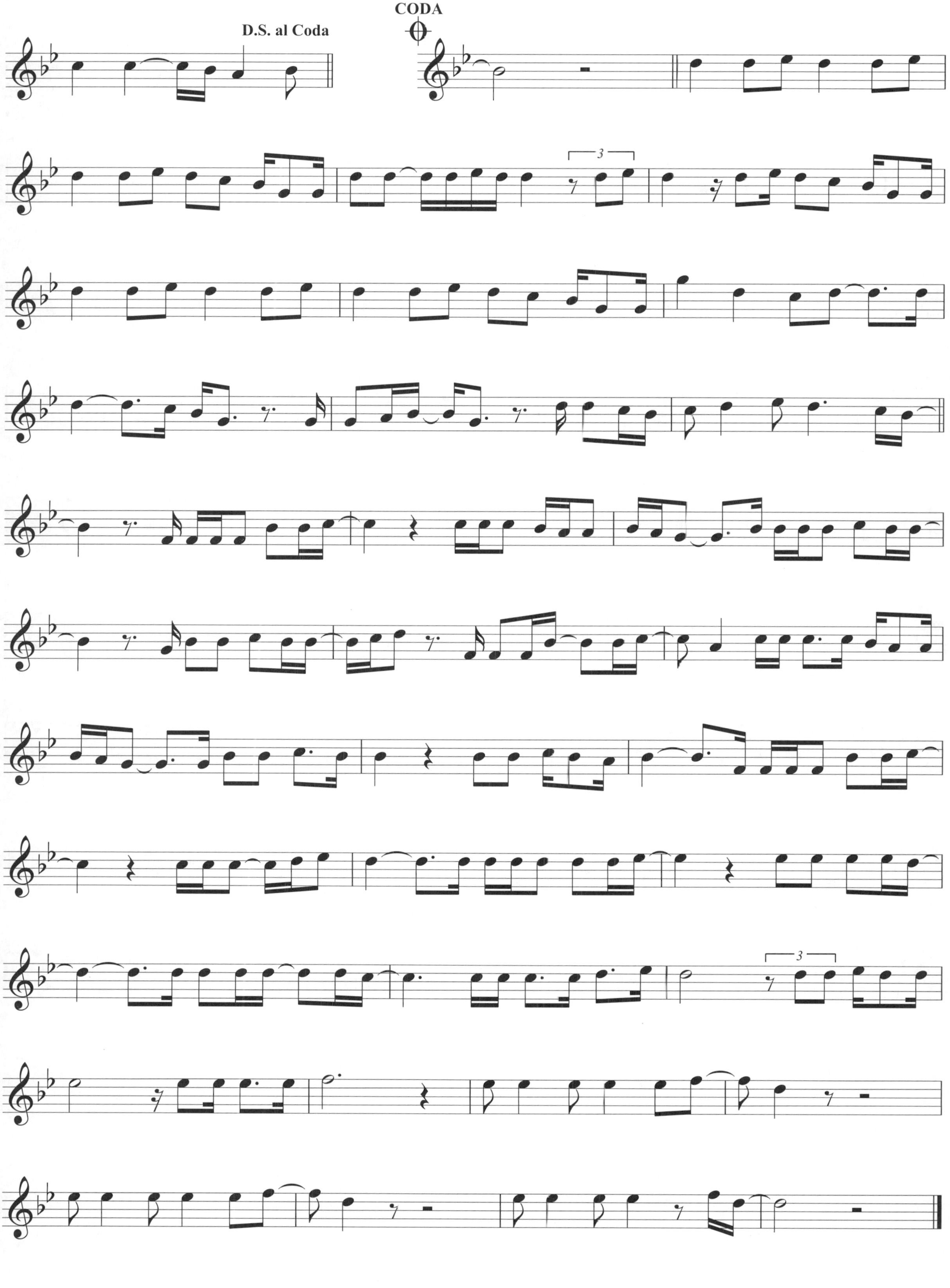
D.S. al Coda
CODA
3
3

JUST THE WAY YOU ARE

TRUMPET

Words and Music by BRUNO MARS, ARI LEVINE, PHILIP LAWRENCE, KHARI CAIN and KHALIL WALTON

To Coda
Fine
D.S. al Coda
CODA
D.S. al Fine

LIPS OF AN ANGEL

TRUMPET

Words and Music by AUSTIN WINKLER,
ROSS HANSON, LLOYD GARVEY, MARK KING,
MICHAEL RODDEN and BRIAN HOWES

1.
2.

LITTLE TALKS

TRUMPET

Words and Music by
OF MONSTERS AND MEN

Moderately

1.
2.

LET IT GO

TRUMPET

Words and Music by JAMES BAY
and PAUL BARRY

NEED YOU NOW

TRUMPET

Words and Music by HILLARY SCOTT,
CHARLES KELLEY, DAVE HAYWOOD
and JOSH KEAR

LOSING MY RELIGION

TRUMPET

Words and Music by WILLIAM BERRY,
PETER BUCK, MICHAEL MILLS
and MICHAEL STIPE

1.
2.

LOVE SONG

TRUMPET

Words and Music by
SARA BAREILLES

Fine
D.S. al Fine

LOVE STORY

TRUMPET

Words and Music by
TAYLOR SWIFT

Moderately

To Coda
1.
2.
D.S al Coda
CODA

MORE THAN WORDS

TRUMPET

Words and Music by NUNO BETTENCOURT
and GARY CHERONE

1.
2.

NO ONE

TRUMPET

Words and Music by ALICIA KEYS,
KERRY BROTHERS, JR. and GEORGE HARRY

Moderately

To Coda
D.S. al Coda
CODA
3

100 YEARS

TRUMPET

Words and Music by
JOHN ONDRASIK

REHAB

TRUMPET

Words and Music by
AMY WINEHOUSE

THE POWER OF LOVE

TRUMPET

Words by MARY SUSAN APPLEGATE
and JENNIFER RUSH
Music by CANDY DEROUGE
and GUNTHER MENDE

1.
2.
Fine
D.S. al Fine
(take 2nd ending)

ROAR

TRUMPET

Words and Music by KATY PERRY,
LUKASZ GOTTWALD, MAX MARTIN,
BONNIE McKEE and HENRY WALTER

Moderately

ROLLING IN THE DEEP

TRUMPET

Words and Music by ADELE ADKINS
and PAUL EPWORTH

ROYALS

TRUMPET

Words and Music by ELLA YELICH-O'CONNOR
and JOEL LITTLE

SAVE THE BEST FOR LAST

TRUMPET

Words and Music by WENDY WALDMAN,
PHIL GALDSTON and JON LIND

SAY SOMETHING

TRUMPET

Words and Music by IAN AXEL,
CHAD VACCARINO and MIKE CAMPBELL

SHAKE IT OFF

TRUMPET

Words and Music by TAYLOR SWIFT,
MAX MARTIN and SHELLBACK

SECRETS

TRUMPET

Words and Music by
RYAN TEDDER

2nd time, to Coda
3rd time, Fine
D.S. al Coda
CODA
D.S. al Fine

SHE WILL BE LOVED

TRUMPET

Words and Music by ADAM LEVINE
and JAMES VALENTINE

SMELLS LIKE TEEN SPIRIT

TRUMPET

Words and Music by KURT COBAIN,
KRIST NOVOSELIC and DAVE GROHL

SOMETHING TO TALK ABOUT
(Let's Give Them Something to Talk About)

TRUMPET

Words and Music by
SHIRLEY EIKHARD

STAY WITH ME

TRUMPET

Words and Music by SAM SMITH,
JAMES NAPIER, WILLIAM EDWARD PHILLIPS,
TOM PETTY and JEFF LYNNE

STACY'S MOM

TRUMPET

Words and Music by CHRIS COLLINGWOOD
and ADAM SCHLESINGER

Medium Rock

STAY

TRUMPET

Words and Music by MIKKY EKKO
and JUSTIN PARKER

Moderately

Fine
3
D.S. al Fine

STRONGER
(What Doesn't Kill You)

TRUMPET

Words and Music by GREG KURSTIN,
JORGEN ELOFSSON, DAVID GAMSON
and ALEXANDRA TAMPOSI

2nd time, to Coda
3rd time, Fine
D.S. al Coda
CODA
D.S. al Fine

TEARS IN HEAVEN

TRUMPET

Words and Music by ERIC CLAPTON
and WILL JENNINGS

TEENAGE DREAM

TRUMPET

Words and Music by KATY PERRY,
BONNIE McKEE, LUKASZ GOTTWALD,
MAX MARTIN and BENJAMIN LEVIN

Moderately

THINKING OUT LOUD

TRUMPET

Words and Music by ED SHEERAN
and AMY WADGE

Moderately slow

1.
2.

THIS LOVE

TRUMPET

Words and Music by ADAM LEVINE
and JESSE CARMICHAEL

Moderate Rock

A THOUSAND YEARS

from the Summit Entertainment film THE TWILIGHT SAGE: BREAKING DAWN - PART 1

TRUMPET

Words and Music by DAVID HODGES
and CHRISTINA PERRI

TILL THE WORLD ENDS

TRUMPET

Words and Music by LUKASZ GOTTWALD,
MAX MARTIN, KESHA SEBERT
and ALEXANDER KRONLUND

Moderately fast

4th time, to Coda
1.
2.
D.C. al Coda
(take repeat)
CODA

UPTOWN FUNK

TRUMPET

Words and Music by MARK RONSON,
BRUNO MARS, PHILIP LAWRENCE, JEFF BHASKER, DEVON GALLASPY,
NICHOLAUS WILLIAMS, LONNIE SIMMONS, RONNIE WILSON,
CHARLES WILSON, RUDOLPH TAYLOR and ROBERT WILSON

Moderately

1.
2.
To Coda
D.S. al Coda
(take repeat)
CODA

VIVA LA VIDA

TRUMPET

Words and Music by GUY BERRYMAN,
JON BUCKLAND, WILL CHAMPION
and CHRIS MARTIN

WAITING ON THE WORLD TO CHANGE

TRUMPET

Words and Music by
JOHN MAYER

WE CAN'T STOP

TRUMPET

Words and Music by MILEY CYRUS,
THERON THOMAS, TIMOTHY THOMAS, MICHAEL WILLIAMS,
PIERRE SLAUGHTER, DOUGLAS DAVIS and RICKY WALTERS

Moderately slow

WE BELONG TOGETHER

TRUMPET

Words and Music by MARIAH CAREY,
JERMAINE DUPRI, MANUEL SEAL, JOHNTA AUSTIN,
DARNELL BRISTOL, KENNETH EDMONDS, SIDNEY JOHNSON,
PATRICK MOTEN, BOBBY WOMACK and SANDRA SULLY

To Coda
D.S. al Coda
CODA

WE FOUND LOVE

TRUMPET

Words and Music by
CALVIN HARRIS

WHAT MAKES YOU BEAUTIFUL

TRUMPET

Words and Music by SAVAN KOTECHA,
RAMI YACOUB and CARL FALK

WHEN YOU SAY NOTHING AT ALL

TRUMPET

Words and Music by DON SCHLITZ
and PAUL OVERSTREET

YOU RAISE ME UP

TRUMPET

Words and Music by BRENDAN GRAHAM
and ROLF LOVLAND

YEAH!

TRUMPET

Words and Music by JAMES PHILLIPS,
LA MARQUIS JEFFERSON, CHRISTOPHER BRIDGES,
JONATHAN SMITH and SEAN GARRETT

1.
2.
Fine
D.S. al Fine
(take repeat)

YOU WERE MEANT FOR ME

TRUMPET

Words and Music by JEWEL MURRAY
and STEVE POLTZ

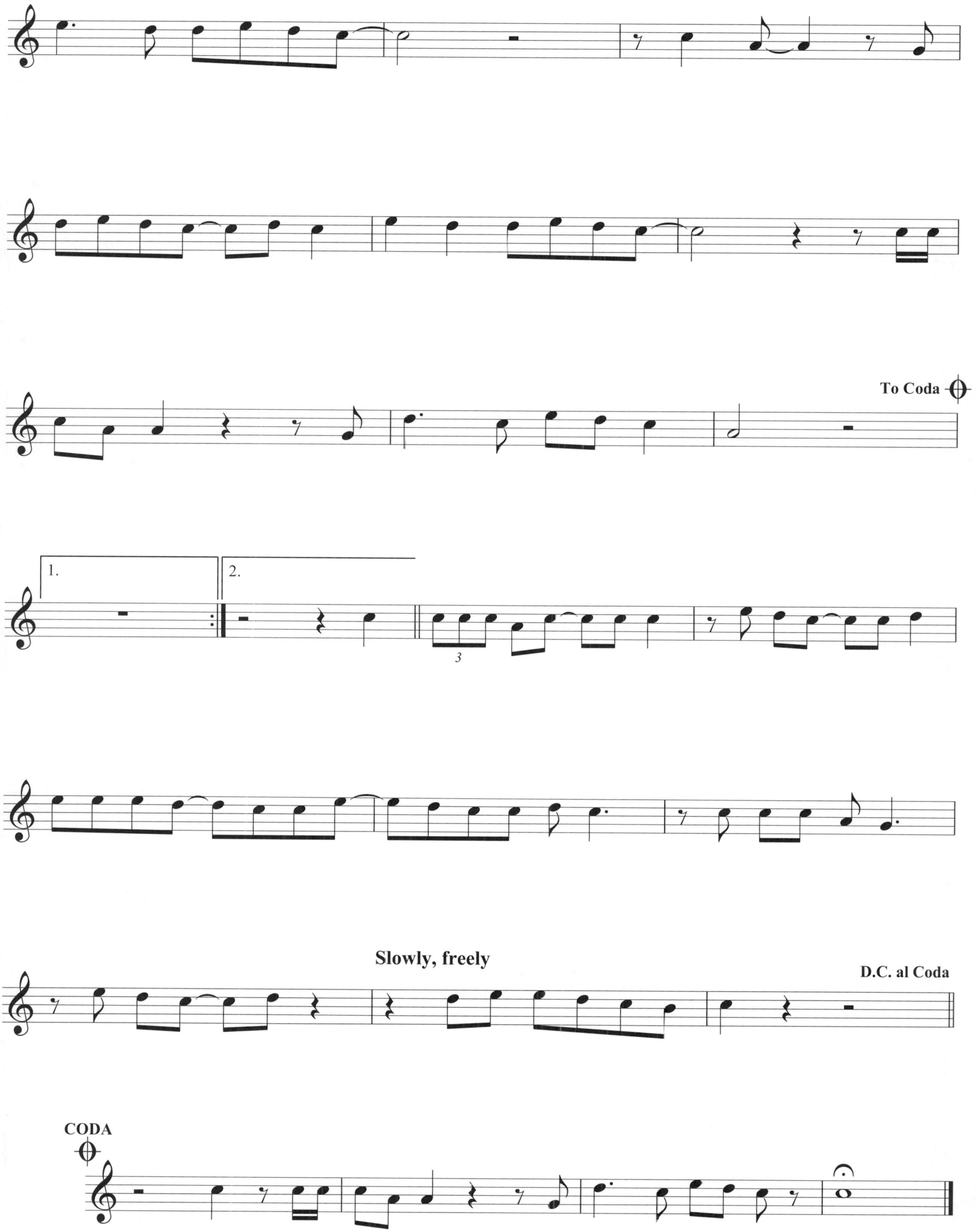
To Coda
1.
2.
3
Slowly, freely
D.C. al Coda
CODA

YOU'RE BEAUTIFUL

TRUMPET

Words and Music by JAMES BLUNT,
SACHA SKARBEK and AMANDA GHOST

YOU'RE STILL THE ONE

TRUMPET

Words and Music by SHANIA TWAIN
and R.J. LANGE

YOU'VE GOT A FRIEND IN ME

from Walt Disney's TOY STORY

TRUMPET

Music and Lyrics by
RANDY NEWMAN

101 SONGS

BIG COLLECTIONS OF FAVORITE SONGS
ARRANGED FOR SOLO INSTRUMENTALISTS.

101 BROADWAY SONGS

00154199 Flute..............$15.99
00154200 Clarinet.......$15.99
00154201 Alto Sax........$15.99
00154202 Tenor Sax....$16.99
00154203 Trumpet.......$15.99
00154204 Horn.............$15.99
00154205 Trombone...$15.99
00154206 Violin...........$15.99
00154207 Viola..$15.99
00154208 Cello..$15.99

101 DISNEY SONGS

00244104 Flute.............$17.99
00244106 Clarinet.......$17.99
00244107 Alto Sax.......$17.99
00244108 Tenor Sax...$17.99
00244109 Trumpet.......$17.99
00244112 Horn...............$17.99
00244120 Trombone...$17.99
00244121 Violin..............$17.99
00244125 Viola..$17.99
00244126 Cello..$17.99

101 MOVIE HITS

00158087 Flute.............$15.99
00158088 Clarinet.......$15.99
00158089 Alto Sax......$15.99
00158090 Tenor Sax...$15.99
00158091 Trumpet........$15.99
00158092 Horn.............$15.99
00158093 Trombone...$15.99
00158094 Violin...........$15.99
00158095 Viola..$15.99
00158096 Cello..$15.99

101 CHRISTMAS SONGS

00278637 Flute.............$15.99
00278638 Clarinet.......$15.99
00278639 Alto Sax......$15.99
00278640 Tenor Sax..$15.99
00278641 Trumpet........$15.99
00278642 Horn.............$14.99
00278643 Trombone...$15.99
00278644 Violin...........$15.99
00278645 Viola..$15.99
00278646 Cello..$15.99

101 HIT SONGS

00194561 Flute...............$17.99
00197182 Clarinet..........$17.99
00197183 Alto Sax........$17.99
00197184 Tenor Sax.....$17.99
00197185 Trumpet..........$17.99
00197186 Horn...............$17.99
00197187 Trombone.....$17.99
00197188 Violin.............$17.99
00197189 Viola..$17.99
00197190 Cello..$17.99

101 POPULAR SONGS

00224722 Flute.............$17.99
00224723 Clarinet.......$17.99
00224724 Alto Sax......$17.99
00224725 Tenor Sax...$17.99
00224726 Trumpet.......$17.99
00224727 Horn.............$17.99
00224728 Trombone...$17.99
00224729 Violin...........$17.99
00224730 Viola..$17.99
00224731 Cello..$17.99

101 CLASSICAL THEMES

00155315 Flute..............$15.99
00155317 Clarinet.........$15.99
00155318 Alto Sax........$15.99
00155319 Tenor Sax.....$15.99
00155320 Trumpet.......$15.99
00155321 Horn...............$15.99
00155322 Trombone....$15.99
00155323 Violin.............$15.99
00155324 Viola..$15.99
00155325 Cello..$15.99

101 JAZZ SONGS

00146363 Flute.............$15.99
00146364 Clarinet........$15.99
00146366 Alto Sax.......$15.99
00146367 Tenor Sax....$15.99
00146368 Trumpet.......$15.99
00146369 Horn.............$14.99
00146370 Trombone...$15.99
00146371 Violin.............$15.99
00146372 Viola..$15.99
00146373 Cello..$15.99

101 MOST BEAUTIFUL SONGS

00291023 Flute.............$16.99
00291041 Clarinet.........$16.99
00291042 Alto Sax........$17.99
00291043 Tenor Sax.....$17.99
00291044 Trumpet.......$16.99
00291045 Horn..............$16.99
00291046 Trombone...$16.99
00291047 Violin............$16.99
00291048 Viola..$16.99
00291049 Cello..$17.99

See complete song lists and sample pages at www.halleonard.com

HAL•LEONARD®
www.halleonard.com

Prices, contents and availability subject to change without notice.

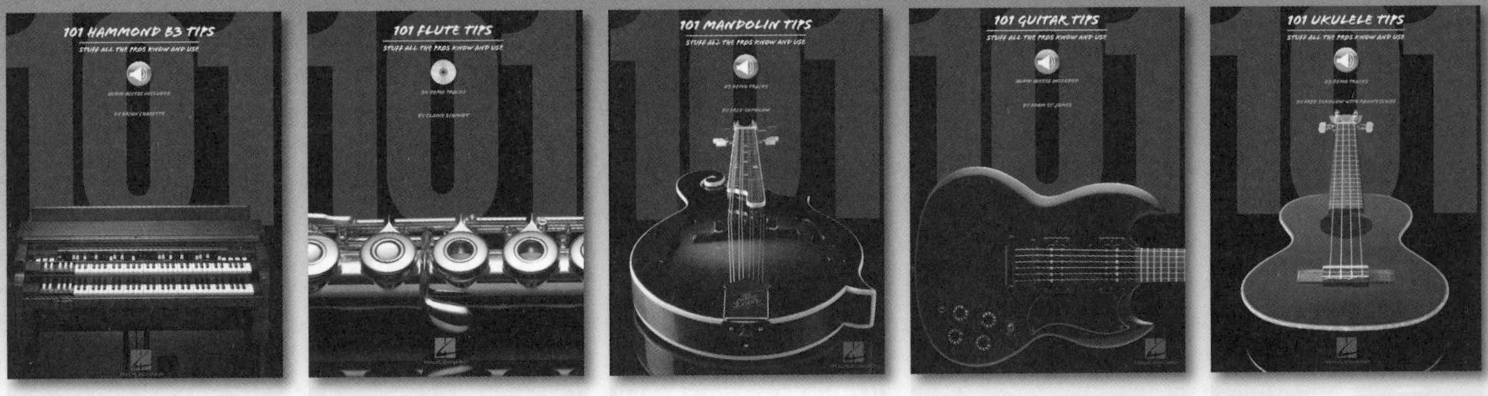

101 HAMMOND B3 TIPS
101 FLUTE TIPS
101 MANDOLIN TIPS
101 GUITAR TIPS
101 UKULELE TIPS